T0164469

Planted by the Signs

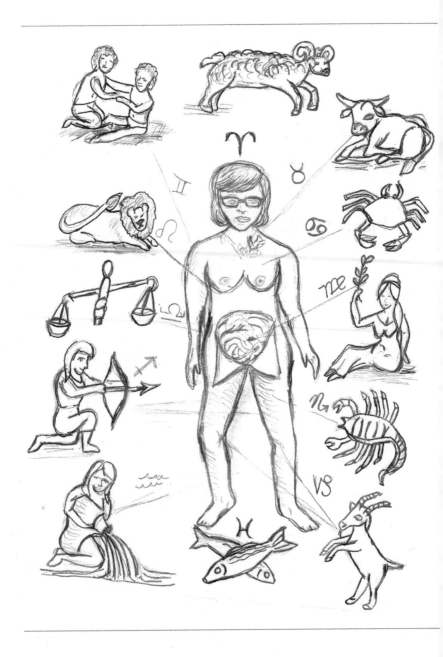

Planted by the Signs

poems

Misty Skaggs

#ohiouniversitypress

#athensohio

Ohio University Press, Athens, Ohio 45701
ohioswallow.com
© 2019 by Misty Skaggs
All rights reserved

To obtain permission to quote, reprint, or otherwise reproduce
or distribute material from Ohio University Press publications,
please contact our rights and permissions department at
(740) 593-1154 or (740) 593-4536 (fax).

All illustrations by author. ©2019 by Misty Skaggs

Printed in the United States of America
Ohio University Press books are printed on acid-free paper ⊗ ™

29 28 27 26 25 24 23 22 21 20 19   5 4 3 2 1

Library of Congress Cataloging-in-Publication Data
Names: Skaggs, Misty, 1982- author.
Title: Planted by the signs : poems / Misty Skaggs.
Description: Athens, Ohio : Ohio University Press, [2019] | Summary:
  "Planted by the Signs brings us the contemporary Appalachian poetry of
  Misty Skaggs. With a knack for pointed personal and social observation,
  she tells the stories of generations of women who have learned to
  navigate a harsh world with a little help from the Farmers' Almanac and
  the stars: women who know how to plant by the signs"-- Provided by
  publisher.
Identifiers: LCCN 2019022594 | ISBN 9780821423813 (paperback ; acid-free
  paper) | ISBN 9780821446805 (pdf)
Subjects: LCSH: Women farmers--Poetry. | Farm life--Poetry. | Appalachian
  Region--Poetry.
Classification: LCC PS3619.K33 A6 2019 | DDC 811/.6--dc23
LC record available at https://lccn.loc.gov/2019022594

These poems are for the generations of

hillbilly women who made me.

Thank you, thank you, thank you.

Contents

Preface   xi

When the Signs Are in the Head

Wet Dew   3
The Home Cemetery   4
Churched   6
I'd Melt   7
Stacking Firewood   8
Oatmeal Cookie Communion   9
Uncle Charlie Loves You   11
Jump Rope Jitters   13
Crying Mad   14
The Strikeout   15
Regenerate   16
Single-Wide Self-Care   17
The Banty Boy   18
Creosote Sunrise   19
Distress Call   20
Election Year   21
Charmed and Charming   22
Timber   23
Lawless   24
The Criminal   25
Heart and Hearth   26
Nighttime Noises   27
Picture Day   28
Small Talk   29
War amid the Cabbage   31
Celestial Midnight Snack   32
Big City Surprise   33

When the Signs Are in the Breast

The Call of the Creek Bank   37
Pulling Plants   38

Peach Blossoms   39
Breaking Beans   40
Kentucky Heat   42
Charlie and Lovel   43
Not Much of a Mommy   45
Babies Having Babies   46
Disconnect   47
The Holy Trinity   48
The Scanner   49
Lovel Gets the Last Word   50
How Not to Act Right   52
Double D Dilemma   53
Ode to the Bethany House   54
Babysitting   55
An Aria for Isonville   56
Daddy Issues   57
You Might Drown   58
Taters and Rainbows   59
Mongrels   60
Roadwork Ahead   61
Royalty   62
Scorpion Tattoo   63
Stubby   64
Honky-Tonk Dreams   65
Mountain Lion   66
Cat Person   67
Goodnight, Gramaw   68
Gooseberries   69
Mommy and Mamaw and Them   70

When the Signs Are in the Reins

Breathing Ghosts   73
In the Dark   75
Bitter Berries   76
Accidents   77
Housefire on 504   79
Bless Her Heart   80

Hard to Swallow   81

The Art of Falling Apart   82

The Rain   83

Going Shedding   84

Super Moon   85

Giveaway   87

Truck Stop Strangers   88

The Lilac Bush   90

Wood Paneling   91

Blooms and the Blood   92

Attempted Escape   93

Funeral Flowers   94

Powerball Power Play   95

From around Here   97

Picnicking with the Dead   99

Preface

At Great Mamaw's house there was always a pone of corn-
bread on the kitchen table. And maybe if you were lucky
some buttermilk biscuits leftover from breakfast. At Great
Mamaw's house there was always something to eat fresh
from the garden. And there was always something to read,
too. It was heaven on earth for a fat little hillbilly word nerd.

There were back issues of *National Geographic* stacked
up in the corner of the living room. A basket of trashy ro-
mance novels with seething, sultry, shirtless men overflowed
next to Great Mamaw's recliner. There was a Kennedy biog-
raphy and a beat-up, flea market copy of *Profiles in Courage*
displayed on the side table right next to her commemorative
presidential plate. The family Bible squatted solemn and thick
and reverent on her nightstand with its gossamer-thin pages
at rest and not to be disturbed by the grubby, clumsy hands
of young'uns. Out in the rusty little camper where she stored
all the scrap material from her quilts, she also stashed the
racy *True Detective* magazines I was never supposed to find.

My favorite book was her favorite book. The one she
made good use of and referred to most often. The book that
Great Mamaw kept tucked in her apron pocket or laid out
within reach, easy to get to on the crooked little coffee table—
The Old Farmer's Almanac. My Great Mamaw lived her life by
the signs. She knew when the moon waxed and waned above
her little holler and she knew what its moods meant for the soil
her roots were planted in.

This collection is inspired by and written for my Great
Mamaw, Lovel Blankenbeckler. It was my honest-to-good-
ness honor to care for her at the end of her life, and many of
the following poems were written during that time. My Great
Mamaw taught me her ways, those ways forgotten and buried
in the pages of the almanac. She taught me to look up at
the sky, to feel the stars move through my body and right on
into the ground. She taught me to know when to plant and
harvest, and she taught me to know when to bloom.

When the Signs Are in the Head

Wet Dew

My place is five fifteen
in the morning
in a plastic lawn chair.
The kind you buy
four for twenty
at the Dollar General.
Flecks of red spray paint
cling to my skin.

The tortoiseshell cat is satisfied
to sleep in the cradle of my legs,
crossed ankle to knee
like a man.
She's making biscuits.
Needlepoint pricks
of practiced country cat claws
kneading my pale, doughy flesh.

The stray shepherd,
one eye sky blue and
the other mud brown,
is never satisfied.
But he missed me
when I ventured off the Ridge
and into town.
So he sits
as patient as he can manage
and I scratch his muzzle
and listen to the knock
of his tail on loose, front-porch
floorboards.

We sit in silence.

Except for the thump and the purr.

Except for the cardinal
screaming
"Wet dew! Wet dew!"
one last time
before the light breaks
the whole holler.

The Home Cemetery

We keep our dead
at the dead end
of a rutted gravel road.
Generations filed away
forever
in staggered rows.

They belong to me.

A birthright of last breath
And rotting body,
buried safely beneath
six feet of soil.
The dark soil

I came from.
Full grown and dirt poor.
This is my acreage.
Rich bottomland fertilized
by bone.

The cemetery floats,
a rounded island tethered
to the mountains
by creek-bed tombstones.
Dusted with broom sage.
Populated solely by lingering souls
and a stray, persistent
peacock
trespassing on my land,
picking his hungry way
over my graves.

Churched

All the old men
from the Beartown
Church of God
call me Sissy.
There's Ligey
and Whirley
and Johnny
and my Mamaw's cousin
who found Jesus
after he beat cancer
a couple years back.

They're working men
of God.
They reminisce
about their drinking days
and trade around trucks
and stories about bad kids
and worsening eyesight.

When they think I'm eighteen,
they grin at the possibilities.
When they find out I'm thirtysomething,
the grins get a little sad
and soft around the edges,
at the thought
of the waste
of a good pair
of breeding hips.

I'd Melt

I want the kind of man
who wants the kind of woman
who keeps bacon grease.
He needs to notice
how it's so much more
than stingy sustenance.
It's ritual and relish,
the satisfaction of golden-brown biscuits.
He has to see

how it's more
than just grease.
It's gumption
and tradition
strained into a coffee cup
passed down through generations.
I need a man to recognize
the kind of love worth saving.
I long for a love
that holds up

like cast iron.

Stacking Firewood

Sticks of seasoned oak
smack the bottom of my wagon
as I whittle away at the woodpile.
Bend and heave, grunt and let fly.
I suck down the coming snow
and fill my lungs so deep it stings.
I find my rhythm,

sweating steam in the cold sunshine.
Bend and heave, grunt and let fly.
I lose it again when I spot a patch
of purple moss worthy of a poem
and take it as a sign,
reward for hard work
turned to smoke.

Oatmeal Cookie Communion

The layered skirttail
brushing my plump, pink,
baby cheek
is plaid.
Skinny strips of harvest orange
and goldenrod yellow
pen in blocks of pea green.
The geometric fields and fences

are flip-flopped.
Planted beneath a swirl of paisley sea.
A housedress,
with every imaginable
blue hue
worn thin with age,
soft and semi-see-through.

The loose skin of the leg
shielded by the layers of cloth
is the same.
Translucent and shimmering
like a clean, cotton sheet
in the spring sunlight
on the clothesline strung
between maple trees out back.

There's a thick, curvy, muscled calf
built up by farming
family bottomland,
tenderized by age and hard work,
and finally gone to seed.
Somewhere above the skirt
and the housecoat
and the apron
and the swirl of color and texture—
somewhere far above the vines
of defined veins easy to trace
with a four-year-old fingertip—
there was a woman.

A tender woman
and a tender, twangy voice
drifting down to me.
Somewhere up there
there were watery blue eyes
and thick plastic glasses
with even thicker lenses.
And a loose white bun
hovered above those
with strands as thin and delicate
as spider silk, escaping
to brush across her wrinkled face.

I stand to receive the homemade
oatmeal cookie communion
she hands down to me.
Her pockets fill my vision and run over.
Slips of paper scribbled
with old-fashioned names
like Vangeline
and Isolene
and Iva
and Lovel.
Horehound candy and sticky peppermints,
white tufts of tissue paper
and the crinkly, plastic wrapper
protecting a plug of King B.

Her face is blurry
in my young memory
but her kitchen is as clear
as the strange shadows
on faded linoleum.
Shadows I liked to watch dance
as I slid across the room
dragging my butt over bumps
and sinkholes settled
into the floor
of an old house in Soldier.

Uncle Charlie Loves You

I remember tired, washed-out women
warning us young'uns
with his name—
"Uncle Charlie's gonna come,
gonna come all the way
out here
just to get you."
I remember we believed it.
I remember the good ol' boys

rounding up a posse
fueled by boredom
and Pabst Blue Ribbon
every damn time
he went up for parole.
He might get out,
he might come home.
No-Name Maddox,
backwoods bastard,
progeny of a prostitute
with no paved streets to walk.
He could've been one of them,
with a Mamaw on Mauk Ridge.
Might've been another nobody
puffed up on Kentucky windage,
bedding high school girls
in the bed of a beat-up
pickup truck
saying,
"I don't know
what *somebody* is."
Or maybe

Uncle Charlie
could've been a country preacher.
A powerful, primitive Baptist
running the church house like a family.
A short feller filled

plumb up to the brim
with rural route righteousness,
briar-hopping the pulpit
instead of hitching to Haight-Ashbury.
The Holy Spirit in his wild eyes
instead of homicide.
I know

I hear Kentucky in his voice.
Hiding in the space
at the ends of words
where consonants drop off
and disappear.

Jump Rope Jitters

I'm still falling down.
Like when I was in fourth grade
and the worst in class at jumping rope.
I can still feel my little kid skin connect
with playground concrete
and see the bright red ribbons of blood
cutting a path to the cuff
of my ruffled pastel socks.
I can still feel loose gravel trapped
right below the surface.
Bits of rock worked their way out
and left rough skin behind.
I can hear the skim and skip
and my heart speeds up to keep up.
The matching scars on my knees itch

as I lie awake at night.
I know there's no recess to dread tomorrow
and I should be drifting gently
toward a soft sleep, but my legs jerk
and my belly bubbles up with bad nerves
and somehow I'm still falling down.

Crying Mad

Lord, I love to watch a woman get mad,
temper rising in her cheeks like rouge.
It's a beautiful sight to behold,
womankind flushed and furious
when she's had enough
and she's about to tell you so.
Maybe she's scowling,
brows furrowed like plowed ground,
pink tongue scythe sharp
and fixing to mow you down.
Maybe she's happy to be snarling,

with the slightest tremble in her lips,
anticipating pouncing
and the act of eating you alive.
Or maybe she's like me
and there are tears in her eyes
trying in vain
to drown out the flashing wildfire
already blazing far beyond her control.

The Strikeout

We were playin' ball
in the old baccer bottom
over on Bruin
when Mom struck me out
and whipped my ass right there
in front of the birds and the bees
and the whole brood.
I was thirteen
and the hormones were in full swing
and so was my secondhand
Louisville Slugger.
Her underhanded pitch flew fast
and so did my temper.
I charged the mound
and the woman who birthed me.
I saw red and then cloudless blue sky
and Mommy's face, not smug,
but smiling

and hovering above me
as I wriggled in the lush cover crop
flat on my back and fuming
and still not as strong
as she always was.

Regenerate

A blue-tailed lizard skitters in stop motion
over damp sandstone.
Tiny reptile muscles ripple
and reflect raindrop puddles.
The lizard darts through
thickets of clover, dodging the eager claws
of deadly kitten paws.
Those bright, blue tails

are breakable.
A defense mechanism
allowing for easy escape.
Bubby and me used to try and fail
to capture the same creatures,
or ancestors of the same creatures,
creeping up on me over two decades.
Emerging from the hot, gray block
of our childhood home at Bruin.

Trying to snap them up
was a fruitless affair.
Same as sitting on the long-gone steps,
blond heads in the cup of small hands,
staring at a two-lane road and
guessing what color car
would come barreling down Route 7 next.
Once in a while we guessed right
and once in a while

we were quick enough.
Trapping the squirming, bright-blue
back ends of those frantic lizards
with one well-placed pinch.
They'd only slip away,
the pinstriped lizards.
Dapperly detach themselves
from fragile, colorful tails
and disappear.

Single-Wide Self-Care

I scrounge around in the bottom cabinets
and dig out the biggest pots we got.
There's the cooker Great Mamaw uses
for canning green beans
and my deep dumplin' pot.
Together they hold gallons
of podunk pampering.
The water on the stove hits boiling
and I run a bath in the slime green tub,
ignoring the groaning pipes
and getting the better
of the hunk of junk
that's supposed to heat it for me.
It's a tight fit, that trailer tub,
but I haven't cooked myself yet
and nothing beats the luxury
of a brand-new bar of soap.

The Banty Boy

The little boy
who lives one ridge over
has thirty-eight real fancy roosters.
And a guinea and four geese
and a whole damn family
of peafowl
who snack their way across the hollow
to breach the barbed-wire perimeter
and chase our mutt dog
around the spot where the garden goes.

The flashy cocks are confused
without drab-colored hens.
The roosters crow from the crack of dawn
'til the eastern Kentucky sky
burns a western bonfire of orange
and purple and pink.

I sit on the porch
and imagine the banties
with their loud plumage glinting,
taking turns announcing every moment
from daylight to dusk.
I imagine the little boy laughs
at the barnyard blaring
as those roosters crow
and complain.

Creosote Sunrise

The sunrise on Stark Ridge
is spectacular today.
All the right spots on the spectrum
are represented—
crimson edged in magenta,
deep orange and the simmering yellow
of a new day splashed
over cloud-splattered sky.
I want to get lost in it,

but all I can think about is the stovepipe.
And the crackle of creosote.
That phantom, black crackle
rubbing my nerves the wrong way
and tinkling against my eardrums.
That primordial-sounding shit,

the revenge of a stick of wood
gone in too green
and the spirits of sap
scorched out of pine kindling.
Who can look at the sky
and follow the smoke
to the stratosphere
when there's so much dirty work to do
right down here on the ground.

Distress Call

I wish I spoke Morse code
so I could see what that guy
on the scanner has to say.
He's bleeping it up all night—
two, four, six a.m.
He likes to communicate like clockwork,
broadcasting on the even hours.
I'm wide awake and just the opposite,
translating on the odd.
Sometimes I jot it down.
Or try to.
He's just so
damned
fast.
Short long long short.
Or was it

short short long long short?
Bullets and dashes flung out
to stab the cold country air.
Taps on the wall
recalled from the depths
of a childhood bedroom.
I want to understand him,

this stranger
who can't sleep either.
I worry about him,
this stranger
who shares my night.
What if he's in trouble?

Election Year

I had just struggled free
from the confines of my bra
and heaved an unhindered breath
when there was a knock at my door.
I don't usually find visitors smiling
on my front porch out here
where the gravel ends.
It's too far out for the Jehovah's Witnesses.
I let him in, titties flopping,
and the candidate made himself comfy
on our couch.
And he wouldn't drink my coffee.
And he told us about his wife
who insisted the gas tank be filled.
And he didn't get my vote
but he left me wondering
what it might be like
to be the kind of woman
who wouldn't touch a stick of firewood.

Charmed and Charming

Sometimes I dream about bees,
but it's not scary.
The harmonious buzz
of a whole hive
enveloping me.
It's not a nightmare,
the honey-sweet sting
and the beat of wings
as the drones drown out
the world.
As I'm swallowed up
by a swarm
and a swirl of smoke.
In the dream I feel charmed
and charming,
hypnotized
and still.
In the dream
the whole world
has turned to wax.

Timber

The woodstove
dries me out
and leaves me gasping
and sucking down hot air,
filling my lungs
with the smoky smell
of home.
Stacking up the tinderbox
is a hell of a lot cheaper
than paying off the gas man,
fifty dollars at a time
as long as the snow is flying
and falling.
And way on into spring.
The woods on this land—

Great Papaw's land,
family land—
these woods are willing
and able
and eager
to give their lives.
Hickory and oak

falling
and fallen
and ready to be felled.

Lawless

I try to tell
my friends from town
there ain't no law on the Ridge.
No blue lights flashing in your mirrors,
no po-po on patrol.
Just one, wore-out state boy
with three counties to cover
and no overtime pay in sight.
You don't have to worry

about how big your bonfire gets
or how loudly your music echoes
off the foothills
and the hollers.
The neighbors won't call the cops
because there ain't no neighbors
and there ain't no cops
and the sheriff can't be bothered
to gas up the cruiser
more than once a week.

The Criminal

I made it about five minutes
into the local news this morning
before I got all teary eyed
and gritted my teeth so hard
I broke a little piece off that bad one
in the back.
"Now it's no excuse,"
said the visibly shaking criminal,

"no matter how cold it gets."
All I could see were faded jeans
and tennis shoes without socks
and cans of Vienna sausages
in a plastic bag.
Nobody lived there,
but somebody owned it,
that empty house he wandered into
to get out of the freezing rain.
"I'm sorry,"
sputtered the scrawny criminal,
the former student of the man
who went ahead and pressed charges
but kindly returned his shopping cart.
"It will never happen again."

Heart and Hearth

When he left,
he left the stove, at least.
When he lit out,
he left it burning.
Left the coals glowing
and the heat radiating news
of his most recent abandonment.
Left a warm emptiness
for her to discover
when she dragged in home
from a double shift at the sewing factory.

The walls may be as bare as the cabinets
and her heart may be broke
but she feels warm
in a hand-me-down way.
In the plaid jacket Daddy gave her
and her worn-down work shoes
passed to her from Momma.

At least when he left, he left the stove.
It was the heart of the home
to begin with.

Nighttime Noises

I had a good nap today.
The kind where you don't dream
and you don't move
and you wake up confused
because the daytime swapped itself out
for the night.
Dark doesn't really come quiet

to the country.
Crickets and whippoorwills
are waking up too.
Coyotes wail instead of sirens.
I can hear things moving under moonlight
and I doubt I'll have peace before dawn.
Out here, even the stars are loud.

Picture Day

All the children stand still
in 1935.

All save for little Eulah,
third from the left,
fidgeting up a front-row blur.
Distracted by her own ruffled socks
and the "unknown girl with bow"
to her right.
The bow is a floppy, frayed ribbon.
Tied crooked. Tired.
Worked loose.

Beecher is the biggest boy
and the most handsome.
His light hair glitters grease,
slick and sharp
like his smirk
and the starch
in his crisp collared shirt
under overalls.

Everyone
is wearing shoes.

Small Talk

Nobody wants to hear
about my new holler life.
Even though I listen courteously
to classist swill spilled
over organic dinners with vegan options.
My small talk is not spicy
like an authentic curry recipe.
It's mostly salt and pepper.

My anecdotes don't unfold
in smoky bars or seedy truck stops
or one-bedroom flops for misguided,
horny, hillbilly youth.
At least not anymore.

Nobody wants to hear
about bowel movements.
Black and hard.
Lumps of sick coal staining the bowl.

Nobody wants to hear
about caring for a dying woman
who will never be ready
to die.

Or about how her arm hurts
and aches until she screams.
About how I stay up all night
and heat towels to wrap her tired limbs.
About her heart failing,
congestively.
Everybody wants to hear

about how we sit around
and talk smack on Herbert Hoover.
About how she refers to Johnny and June
like family.

Everybody wants to hear
about how she loves to read
the raunchy romances.
The ones with shirtless pirates
or lusty-eyed cowboys on the covers.
But nobody wants to hear

about how sometimes I sit straight up
as I'm drifting off.
And it's *my* heart.

It stops.

And I could swear I can hear her soul
leaving her body
through the baby monitor.

War amid the Cabbage

The garden is plowed
and planting season is in the air,
between snowflakes.
I keep thinking about the time
me and that cutworm went to war.
It was a backyard brawl,

one on one in a raised-bed arena
built from concrete blocks
and designed to coddle my cabbage.
Somewhere buried deep
under all that dirt I packed in
one wheelbarrow load at a time
it lurked.
Mocking me, waiting quietly
in the underground dark
to sabotage my future sauerkraut.
Shoo, you should've seen me
down on my hands and knees
with a sieve and a spoon
sifting slowly through the soil,
working up a sweat
and cussing up a storm
and determined to slay
my solitary, slimy enemy.

Celestial Midnight Snack

I want to take a chunk
out of the moon.
Reach right up and pluck it down
with both my greedy little hands.
It's so full up there
and I'm so hungry here on the ground.
I want the warm, waning feeling
of glowing gluttony
in the pit of my stomach.
I want to swallow all the stars

and leave bite marks
on the lunar surface.
Sink my teeth in because
footprints have been done.

Big City Surprise

I saw a red-tailed hawk
with his red tail flashing
sunlight
lift up off the side
of the highway
right outside Louisville.
He shouldn't have been there,
a bronze bird
like the one who lives
along the weedy, two-track trail
to the graveyard.

He shouldn't have been there,
so majestically out of place.
Hunched up in a shadow
picking at fat rat roadkill
under an overpass.

When the Signs Are in the Breast

When the Signs Are in the Blood

The Call of the Creek Bank

When she stared
up
at the sky,
she couldn't find the moon.
Or her bearings.

Wide-eyed, she took in
a new tract of wilderness.
A wild where the buzz
of hundreds
of voices
took the place
of the buzz
of honeybees in the hive.
And car horns

honked for crickets,
blared for the bullfrogs.

She balanced
on tiptoe
on her secondhand stiletto heels
on the smooth sidewalk.
She balanced and pretended poise,
panache,
pizzazz.

All the while itching
in the ambient dark
to make a break
for the first creek bank she could find.

Pulling Plants

It's early morning.
A before the sun comes up
and the rooster crows
kind of early morning.
But we don't have a rooster.
Just an alarm clock
and a bunch of cats and dogs.
And sleep in our eyes
as we head out the door
and trudge through the dew
toward the big, blue Ford.
A cab and a half
with a bed full of feed sacks.
My baby brother still has a scar

from where the fold-down
backseat nearly bit his thumb off.
But that was a different day.
Today, we're headed
to the tobacco bed
over at Newfoundland.
And the sky is suddenly pink
every time it peeks through the hills
around a curve.

Cutting and hanging
wasn't for the women and the children.
At least not unless the men
were laid up bad
or no-count kind of lazy.

Peach Blossoms

There are peach trees blossoming.
Fluffy sprigs of pink obscured
by the still bare trees
in a thick clump of deep woods
where an old homestead
used to be.
The blossoms are soft.
A fuzzy reminder of future dreams
fallen on hard times.
Finally big enough to bear,

the trees have been forgotten
to sprout forth fat fruit
fallen
to the forest floor.
A feast for the squirrels
and coons and possums.
Low-hanging branches
plucked clean by deer
instead of great-

great-great-grandchildren.
No peach preserves.
No jelly sweet smell
in the air
in a cozy country kitchen.
No kitchen.
But there are still peach trees
blossoming.

Breaking Beans

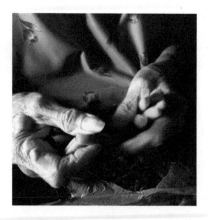

We are an agricultural assembly line.
Weathered human machinery
tucked away under a rusty tin roof.
Sweating and solar powered,
lost in the task at hand.
The front porch hums with
the rhythmic sound
of breaking beans.
Plump, green pods
snap and pop
under the pressure of steady fingers.
Female voices rise and fall
punctuated by a scattered thump,
a handful of Kentucky Wonder
bouncing in the bottom
of a five-gallon bucket.

The sun is sliding down to meet the hills.
We swim in damp evening air.
When it beads and condenses
into fat drops on my upper lip,
I can smell the garden it came from.
And men come up from the garden.

Broad hats and broad backs
wind up a long dirt path
to pause at the front porch.
Delivering pails labeled "Fischer's Lard"
loaded with a tender pick bounty
that spills out around our feet—

Greasy beans and half runners,
bush beans
and turkey beans
and pole beans
and greensleeves.

Kentucky Heat

The sticky Kentucky heat
can't stop you and me
and old man Kessler
from sitting outside in the dark.
We reminisce with fireflies
about how childhoods melt away,
so much ice at the bottom
of a tacky, flea-market tumbler.

And the cheap-ass whiskey
makes our lips get loose.
And that mellow homegrown
makes our talk get sweeter.
And our voices and our feelings,
typically sealed up like a Mason jar,
rise and fall freely
and float
on the summer air.
Lightning bugs hang
over the green hills
that spawned us
and taught us
everything we think
we know.

Charlie and Lovel

He came to pick her up
in a car that cranked.
Thurston, in the Model T
wearing a slick hairdo
and a bow tie, askew.
He was handsome
though stiff and nervous
standing next to a pretty farm girl
in front of the family barn
on a first date
in the forties.

"He's awful handsome!"
I exclaim over this man
who was never her husband.

"I reckon he was," she replied,
nodding with the girlish trace
of a sly grin
on her thin lips.

"How come you didn't marry him?"
I ask, knowing he asked.

She pauses to consider the photo
in the album in front of us.
The couple stands close
but they never touch.
Frozen inches apart forever.

She looks down at me
from her broke-in La-Z-Boy
like I'm plumb ate up
and answers matter-of-factly—

"I didn't love him!"

Every evening
when I help her into bed

and lift her tired legs
onto the feather tick mattress,
she turns to look
longingly
at another picture.

Something more recent,
snapped in the seventies
on a family picnic
down in Cold Spring.
Happiness in the spur of the moment.
No time to pose
for the click
of the camera.

She stares
through the separation
of death
at the two of them, laughing.
Glowing love and wading
ankle-deep in a creek.
His wiry arm wrapped
around her widened waist
eternally.

Not Much of a Mommy

I told Vee, back home
in Kentucky
women said you could walk a baby loose.
They shared stories of grannies and aunties
and double first cousins
leaving puddles along gravel roads
and dirt paths,
muddy signs of new life
they couldn't hold in any longer.
We walked circles around that trailer park.
Especially at dusk, especially at the end.
Vee told me

she wasn't ready to let go,
to release the soul
living so snug inside her.
Vee told me

she wasn't much of a Mommy
but she sure was good
at the being pregnant part.

Babies Having Babies

After twenty-nine hours
of hard labor
all she wanted was a milkshake.
Vanilla.
And maybe a McDouble, too.
When I got there that nasty old man
was all flopped out in her hospital bed.
He posed, baby on his chest,

trying to look parental.
Like he had some part in her ordeal.
I know good and well his part
and it made me cringe.
I strangled a growl and swallowed hard

and forced a smile
and opened my arms wide to her.
After twenty-nine hours of pain,
of pushing and forcing
a screaming new life into this ugly world
she fell against me exhausted
and lamented in my ear
so that he couldn't hear—
"My pussy is pulverized."

Disconnect

The hallway is littered
with loitering twentysomethings,
slouching bodies leaned back
holding up the walls
and hungover.
'Cause it's Friday morning
early
and Thursday night got wild
sipping moonshine, looking down
over a suitcase college town
from the looming party perch
that is Lockegee.
And my eyes flit

back and forth
as I tromp down the hallway,
hoping my steps echo
in their hazy heads.
My eyes land

on the stiff singularity
of proper posture
and a hot pink coat
and a flat face, sad eyes set deep
and drifting off
a thousand and more miles away.
She wasn't there last night
or any other night.

The Holy Trinity

When my Papaw died
I was reading a biography
of Edgar Cayce.
He was the farmer prophet,
the hillbilly healer.
An old soul born again in the backwoods
and visited by angels
on the creek bank.

The night we planted my Papaw
in the plot he picked out
I sat sweating
in the porch swing,
thick book in my thick lap.
I swatted fat mosquitoes
and envisioned Edgar as a boy.

Bug-eyed Edgar playing with past lives
in a field full of black-eyed daisies.
Little Edgar with his bulbous head
and his Coke bottle lenses
and his strange, strange ways.
Edgar reading the Bible
to the bluegrass fairies
and the ghost of the girl
out the road.

He came to me on a breeze
laced with Brut.
Papaw, not Edgar.
The smell of him landed at my shoulder.
I felt his soul as familiar
as the weight
of his crippled right hand.
The mangled right hand
he had wanted to remove
with a rusty ax
when it offended him.
And his God.
And Edgar's God, too.

The Scanner

I could write a whole book of poems
about Mamaw's police scanner.
Certain tones perk my ears
like I'm Pavlov's hungry hound dog,
drooling for good gossip,
for juicy scraps of stories tossed out
onto the airwaves to land
in my living room late at night.
I'm listening and wondering
whatever happened to that poor woman
whose husband shot her in the foot
while he was cleaning his forty-five.
I'm listening and lamenting
the thirty-five-year-old female
overdosed and unresponsive,
because in a town this small
I must have known her

or at least known of her.
I'm up at all hours and I'm listening,
filling in the details
with poetic license and abandon
and hoping the two men talking dirty
in the drive-thru at McDonald's
got their asses whipped good
'cause someone bigger
and badder than me
is listening too.

Lovel Gets the Last Word

The living room Papaw built
sprouting from the tiny trailer
leans downhill
toward the garden.
Slightly sloped furniture is arranged
around a big-screen teevee,
three foot thick,
Mamaw got on credit
from the Fingerhut catalog.

Papaw is gone.
And we're the last inhabited homestead
at the end of a road
off a road
off the blacktop.
But even the Mamaws and me
watch the Derby
Especially since coverage pre-empted
our evening dose of local news
and weather.

Tony Cavalier doesn't have to tell me
there's a storm brewing in the sky
over the eKy,
but the sun is shining
on our tin roof and
on the million-dollar hides
of thoroughbreds.

Before the race,
I set out for the back porch
in search of a rainbow
and my secondhand flash.
I want to spice up my sweet instant coffee
and toast debauchery and bourbon
and all those people drinking
dark, aged, potent liquor blood
of the place I love.

To bourbon! Yum!
And betting the whole wad
on a speckled horse.

"He looks like clouds,
galloping," Mamaw remarks.
"And there's our old, ugly governor,"
Great Mamaw replied.
"And his old,
ugly
wife."

How Not to Act Right

He's huffing
and puffing
and plumb mad
and soaked straight through.
He's irritated
down to the bone.
The salt-and-pepper poof
of his teased-up combover
has done gone flat.
He's dripping sweat
and summer rain
and the gold chain and cross
cradled in his damp nest
of chest hair
is turning green,
oozing oxidized meanness
and the gospel
according to him—
"You don't go to a hillbilly church

and call out
to Mohammed!"
He's dripping spit
and summer rain
and I'm saying silent prayers
to every by-god god
I can think of.
He's ranting and raving
and I'm mumbling mantras,
chanting litanies,
reciting rosaries,
flat-out praying for lightning
to strike.
Some folks don't know
how to act right.

#plantedbythesigns

Double D Dilemma

I been battling my bra
for the last two weeks
and it's winning.
I keep finding black-and-blue bruises.
Delicate and sore and mottling
the milky landscape
of my breasts.
It hurts.
Stripes and pinpricks

and lacy contusions left behind
by a day of being locked away.
I want to scream—
"Damn the man!"
and "Damn Maidenform!"
and "Damn these luscious jugs of mine!"
I want to let out
a string of cuss words
that could peel paint
and proceed to peel off
the offending undergarment
and burn that bitch.
But mercy, my back does hurt.

Ode to the Bethany House

There are three brick buildings
squatting in a circle on a hill above town.
One of them is falling in.
Blank windows look at me
with clarity.
All their glassiness is long gone.
The crumbling building,
the tallest building,
I imagine it drops its bricks.
Bricks the color of creek rock

dug out of a clay bank somewhere
not far from here
and fired in a factory that died
and took a whole town with it
when it went.
My favorite junk store

and the local food bank
are located in the shortest building,
the stoutest building.
And today it smells like overripe melon.
Cantaloupes and honeydew
spilling out from busted cardboard boxes.
And the sweet stink stirs around in stale air
all mixed up with mothballs.

Babysitting

I was standing at the sink
washing dinner dishes
when the Daddy talk hit me
right out of nowhere.
I kept my grasp on the glassware
and turned to watch my cousin's little girl
picking at a microwaveable pizza,
sipping some chocolate milk
through a crazy straw
and casually digging up questions
grown people spend a lifetime
trying to pry loose.
I wipe my wet hands

on the tail of my T-shirt
and join her at the table.
In my experience,
it's the best place to explain
to a wide-eyed six-year-old
she was born into a woman's world.

An Aria for Isonville

I wish you'd sing to me.
Throw your head back
and part your lips
and candidly belt out
the unexpected.
The strikingly beautiful notes
of an aria I recognize
but only vaguely.
Maybe *Faust*?
You know it

from the diaphragm
and beyond.
A song completely unfamiliar
to its setting,
out of place
in time and place,
soaring high
and elegant
above the gymnasium floor
at Isonville Elementary.
Notes shaped sweet
and powerful
seeking escape
through the slatted windows
and bouncing
louder than any damn basketball
ever dared.
Remember when
you used to sing?

Daddy Issues

I'm here for the broken girls
and the grown-ass women
who never had a Daddy
and never needed one.
I'm here for the bad bitches
with loud voices
refusing to be silenced.
The ones who might have been princesses.
Heaven forbid.
Confined to fancy balls
and marital beds
and the beauty parlors
of the patriarchy.
If only Daddy had been around
to oversee things properly
and make sure they smiled.
I'm one of those women

brought up by women
who brought home the bacon
and fried it up
and saved the grease for hard times.
The man I never called Daddy
brought me a present once.
A Cabbage Patch doll, missing her papers,
and the bottom half of a bright green
glass bottle of Mountain Dew
and a single Reese's Cup.
While I was getting dressed up,
done up like a curly headed, itty-bitty
blond porcelain doll,
he got hungry along the way.

You Might Drown

If you try and convince me
you can't smell the rain coming
I'm liable to conclude
You're full of shit.
Or else I'd shake my head
and bless your heart
in the judgey kind of way.
It's hard to imagine existing

with your nose stuck in the air
and not a clue what the wind
is trying to tell you.
Listen. The rain crows
are cooing soft warnings
as they pick through the grass
waiting for the worms to wake up.
Look. Every little leaf
turns its pale belly skyward.
There's a storm coming
and they're ready to drink it all in.

Taters and Rainbows

I chased rainbows across two counties.
First out in Farmers
then coming down Christy Creek
and around the ridge,
driving between rural route raindrops.
The kind that leave the blacktop
breathing steam.
I was sure I'd catch up with one
as I topped Merdie Waddell hill
where the light likes to play
in among the broom sage.
But I just missed it.
And followed a black cloud

around the curves, still feeling gracious
that the garden got good and wet.
Taters are more tangible than rainbows.

Mongrels

I used to love to love the lowlifes.
The damaged strays.
The downright dirty lipstick dicks
disguised as decent dudes.

I longed to soothe the rabid.
Gently foaming at the mouth,
swollen tongues lolling out
with a thirst that can't be quenched.
Strays too scared to stay,
terrified to drink from my deep well.

I was always too tempted
to take them in.
The strays who wander up
in the yard at four a.m.
hungry and sniffing around my backdoor.

Roadwork Ahead

The road is in pieces.
Busted up and broken,
scraped down
to bare bones
and ready for a slick coat
of tar.
The honeysuckle smell
that hangs in the humid air
around here
has been overpowered.
Smothered out by the hot stink
of asphalt.
I stop
and crank the windows up
against the chemical breeze,
and the classic rock station

is blaring a song
that reminds me I'm getting old.
I'm mesmerized
by the scrawny stick of a woman
standing in front of me
fighting a reflective sign
bigger than she is.
Her mascara is running
and she's flipping her sweaty ponytail
and tryin' hard to look cute
in a neon vest.
She's tryin' hard
for the menfolk driving by
in their trucks
in the middle of nowhere
going slow
with no destination in mind.

Royalty

I'm trying to think of how to put it,
the way she held reluctant court
with a bunch of strangers

who didn't dare to look away.
They weren't exactly entranced
or charmed by her filthy mouth
and the greasy swath of her hair.
Her stories weren't clever or witty
and almost all of them
started out with cheap vodka
and ended up with a night in jail.
Or the emergency room.
It was all too damned uncomfortable.
The way she splayed open

her gory, gritty insides
for everyone to see
and punctuated sentences
with bloody spit.
You couldn't help but pay attention

the way she commanded it.
The decree of a tragic, trailer park queen
strutting around in jean shorts.

Scorpion Tattoo

The limp, pink leg
of her velour sweatpants
dragged and danced
over the bumpy parking lot.
Empty.
She was fast in that chair.
Her stringy hair caught the wind
she created in her wake

and tangled.
The scorpion
tattooed on her neck
twitched with the effort,
crawling into her ear
and into my memory.
A cigarette dangled from her lips.
The lumps and dips in the pavement
were no obstacle

and her scarred arms
propelled her,
tanned and strained
with lean muscle.
She lost her leg
somewhere along the way
and obviously
she didn't give a shit.
It might have been slowing her down.

Stubby

It's easy
to make hospital buddies.
People are ready to talk,
ready to spill out
all the infectious words.
MRSA and fasciitis
drop off the tongues of loved ones.
Myopathy and ischaemia
and dysphagia
and dementia.
Big words voiced
in country accents.
Over at the park

I go to stretch my legs
and read a book
in the shade of a Chinese maple
and chain-smoke cheap cigarettes
and watch that squirrel
who only has half a tail left.
Me and my hospital pals call him Stubby.
Sometimes I swipe a wheelchair
from the front desk

and push the little old lady
in the plaid quilted jacket
to her own spot, under the oaks.
She's just so tired
and it's the first time
she's gotten off her feet all day.
And her husband ain't getting no better.
Bless his heart.
She says the doctor
keeps talking amputation.
She says maybe
she'll call him Stubby, too.
And she laughs till she coughs
and we talk big about quitting
all the way back up to the fourth floor.

Honky-Tonk Dreams

I can hear birds singing
and smell coffee brewing
in our crooked little kitchen.
A square of light trickles in
through the tiny trailer window.
The morning is here
but I'm having trouble
finding my feet
and getting up on them.
Three times

I yank my quilt back up.
All the way up
over my head.
I can hear birds singing
but my brain feels hazy with whiskey
and cigarette smoke
and sawdust and sorrow
and I know
I been having
those high lonesome,
honky-tonk dreams again.

Mountain Lion

I felt like a predator, a big cat
on the hunt as he bent over
to pop the rusted-out hood
of a nineteen-sixty-something Chevy.
He went on excitedly
in a thick sorghum accent,
a touch of sweet sure
to wind up bitter and lingering
on the back of my tongue.
Wildflowers forced their way up

through the engine block
and framed his baby-fresh face.
Between the way those Wranglers fit
and the way he smiled at me
out there in a secret junkyard
in the middle of the woods,
I might even have licked my lips
before I pounced.

Cat Person

I'm scared to slam the car door.
Even though I enjoy
the middle-of-nowhere echo.
The invasive bang
bouncing off the bareness
of shedding, fall hillsides.

But I can already hear Hank
whining, guttural and angry.
Crouched on the other side
of the screen door.
Hissing and spitting out
the nasty-tasting announcement
of my arrival.

Hank hates me and it hurts my feelings.
I'm a cat person and she's immune
to my feline wiles.
She doesn't purr in response
to the sweet sounds
of my kittykittykitty coos.
Unless she's in heat.

Hank is puffed out,
pissed off, about half feral.
A domestic beast lurking
in the soft-smelling shadows
of a clean, country home.

Goodnight, Gramaw

At two in the morning, I kneel
at the altar
of her rust-brown recliner.
After the credits roll on
past *The Big Valley*
and Miss Barbara Stanwyck
has her hearty last laugh
I fill a plastic pan
packed home from the hospital
with lukewarm city water
and Epsom salts.
How much of this land
sank between her toes?

Through the camphor stink
of white liniment
my soft hands find
where rough heels used to be.
The kind that accompany hard work
and shoes with soles
worn thin.

The medicine burns
my gnawed-up nails.
The effort of her smile
tingles.
"You've got Pap's hands,"
she whispers a blessing.
"All palm and no fingers."

Gooseberries

The gooseberry bush
is hanging full,
thorny branches drooping
under the weight of a tart snack
damned near gone extinct.
We don't care if it stings,
the occasional thorn
finding soft finger pads.
We cultivate the wild

in our big backyard.
We tend to it out behind the shed.
Me and Mamaw,
we keep the taste of yesterday
biting on our tongues.

Mommy and Mamaw and Them

I loved to listen
to Mommy and Mamaw and them
sitting out on the porch of the evening
breaking beans and telling stories
or shucking corn and sharing gossip.
Didn't much matter the task at hand,
the result was rural route sorority.
Women in their element,
loving every minute of it
and daring the sun to sink any lower
on their conversation.
Mamaw's laugh would come
from the ground up, make her whole body
and the foundation shake
when her feisty blonde younger sister
let fly a cussword
they'd have quarreled at the boys over.
Mommy smiled at the scene

and hummed along to an old country song
spinning around somewhere in her head.
There was always something to do
and the women all lit in and went to it,
their calloused hands kept busy,
getting things done.
There was always a row to hoe,
a supper to cook,
a man whose britches and ego
required mending.
There were children and livestock to tend
and Mommy and Mamaw and them
pecked around like a whole pack
of mother hens on the prowl.
Of the evening they'd roost
out on the porch
to cluck in comfort for a while
before that damned cock crowed again.

When the Signs Are in the Reins

Breathing Ghosts

I am haunted
by old-fashioned ways.
I am rooted too deep
to till it all up
and turn over.
I'll never be a transplant

blooming out
in a rooftop garden
or flourishing in foreign soil.
I am the prodigal seed.
Dandelion fluff finding
a way back
to where it began.
I may drift

but I'll always land
in the hills, in the boonies,
in Kentucky.
Carried by a current
of homesickness
coming in chronic, reliable waves.
Here I breathe deep
and do my best

and know my mission.
Here I feel the ghosts
of generations
of family.
Kinfolks filtered
into my lungs
off the country air.
Familiar ghosts send chills
up my spine because sometimes
it's dark that way.
And scary.

Because roots can get tangled.
They can smother out
anything else
that dares
to grow close.

In the Dark

It's late and I'm lonesome.
Even the moon took off on me tonight,
drifted outside of my orbit
and left me behind, staring up
into a sky so black and heavy
it might just droop and sag
and smother the whole holler.
There aren't any stars tonight.
Their bright lights twinkled out
when they noticed me, so small,
barefooted and vulnerable
and calling to them
from down on the ground.
It's late and I'm lonesome

here in the dark
suffering a celestial cold shoulder.

Bitter Berries

The last blackberries of the year
were hanging right there
off an unexpected brier sprung up
underneath the kitchen window.
There were a few good fat ones, too.
Glowing dark and lush
against the battered underpinning.
They mocked me beautifully
after I'd scoured two ridges
foraging hard, desperate to find a pie
along the dirt road.
I never can seem
to keep ahead of the critters.
Eager, I tromped down the grass

and picked them all.
Careful not to drop a one.
Forgetful of bare feet
and lurking copperheads.
I popped a whole handful into my mouth
and I puckered up tight
and let out a shout that slammed
against the cliffs
and scattered a flight of doves.

Accidents

I am hunkered down,
hiding.
Curled into a ball
at the bottom
of a refrigerator box
in the stuffy back bedroom
of Mamaw's mobile home,
wondering what it feels like
to die
at the bottom of a well.

The accident happened
a couple weeks back
and now there's Baby Jessica.
We're almost the same age.
I might let her play
with my Cabbage Patch doll
if she lived out the road.
And if she wasn't snooty.

But she can't play, anyways.
She's stuck.
With mud and muck and darkness
caked in her fine, yellow hair.
For the first time
in my short, heathen life
I pray.
I pray and pray

she won't die
the way my cousins did.
In the black dirt, face down.
In a cold puddle
gasping for air
after digging all day
for clean water
and waiting on an ambulance
that got lost along the way.

I know what I'm doing
is morbid
and wrong.
But I try to block out all the light.
Except for a single, reassuring strand
filtering down between box flaps.
I hope no one will find me

and spank my hind end.
And tell me again
and again—
accidents are real,
accidents happen.
I wonder

if anyone told Jessica.
Maybe she just didn't listen.
I try to block out happy noises
from up the hall
and hold my breath
until I feel faint.

Housefire on 504

The sun hasn't crept up
over the ridge just yet
and somebody's house is burning.
Panicked voices crackle out
from Mamaw's police scanner
and broken phrases like
"fully engulfed"
bring to mind heat and flame
and I feel safe right here

in the dark,
elbow-deep in dishwater
and covered in cold chills.

Bless Her Heart

"Well! Did you hear that one?"
She hollers excitedly from the front room
on into the kitchen
where I'm washing my way
through two sinks full of dishes
and getting my belly soaking wet.
"What'd I miss, Mamaw?"
I holler back.

It must be a good'un
since she puts down her sewing
and gets out of her plush recliner
to scamper into the kitchen—
"Shoo! Lordy! Some poor girl's got shot
down at Hogtown."
And this one is juicy and bloody

so I wipe my wet hands
on my wet shirt
and we sit at the table with a mug apiece
and speculate on circumstance
and wonder if she'll make it.
Bless her heart.

Hard to Swallow

I used to start my mornings
with a cup of coffee and the news.
I'd settle into my favorite chair
and scan the channels
looking for the local weather
and bracing myself for big headlines.
Don't get me wrong, I didn't trust it.
But I watched it.
And I imagined myself clever enough

to sift through the facts
and the copy brought to you by Pfizer.
The news used to make me
sad and skeptical.
Nowadays, I'm just pissed.
Now I start my mornings with coffee
and a Kentucky sunrise,
sitting on the porch
and savoring the bitter taste on my tongue
'cause there ain't enough sugar on earth
to get me to swallow all that bullshit.

The Art of Falling Apart

Backwoods women have perfected the art
of falling apart without a fuss.
Our panic and pain are private,
sealed up tight and put away.
You won't hear our tears
leaking out from behind closed doors.
They aren't meant for you.
We're too busy holding it all together

to indulge in the pleasures
of falling apart.
It can never be a public performance
followed by a rose bouquet.
And we're too greedy
to rip off a piece and share sorrows.
Our sorrow is our own.
You wouldn't understand it anyway.

#plantedbythesigns

The Rain

The rain is here.
I heard the wind that brought it in,
brazen and gusty and bold,
whistling at me
through a drafty window.
The rain recognizes me,
and its rhythms satisfy
my sudden lust for hard refrain.
The rain, the rain.
Fat drops beat out a steady smack

on the tin roof, one at a time.
Stubborn individuals stand out
before they slide away
to be soaked up by soft earth
and thirsty roots.
The rain is here
right below the surface.

Going Shedding

I dreamt of an abandoned building
raised in creek rock
and left to rot.
The foundation was solid
but kudzu took the roof
and covered the windows.
Vines and shade climbed three stories.
I was invited inside

and found the place alive.
Massive luna moths
dangled like chandeliers.
Someone was brewing coffee.
All the empty rooms buzzed
with the voices of women
dressed in white
looking to get shed of their men.

#plantedbythesigns

Super Moon

Maybe we're all just cosmic mush,
she thought.
She stood in the dark
of the holler
alone
and looked up
and up at the uninterrupted sky.
She felt the humid air catch
and hang
in the wet, pink insides
of her throat.

Suspended.

Maybe it's that fucking moon's fault,
she thought.
And she felt a rusty, red clot
passing
through her most sensitive parts,
making her weak at the knees
with the power of it all.
The primordial, copper stank
of potential life deposited
in a pair of granny panties.
Maybe we're all just cosmic mush,

malleable to the moods
of the super moon.
The woods around her
are all lit up.
Possums and skunks and raccoons
creep through the underbrush,
nocturnal entities taken aback
by the light,
cautious.
But the deer are wide awake
at an odd hour
and they snap twigs
for the super moon.
In thanks.

The woman alone
in the clearing next to the garden
doesn't waver.
She stares
into the pale, pockmarked face
in the sky.
And she wonders
if the animals can smell her,
if all that backwoods bullshit
about black bears
sniffing out a woman on the rag
is true.

Maybe we're all
just moonstruck mush,
pulled toward the fickle glow.

Giveaway

We stopped at a yard sale
in Sandy Hook, in the empty lot
where Clete's grocery store used to be.
The brash secondhand saleswoman
started going on to her cousin
in the hot pink tube top
about how she won
one of them big umbrellas
from WSAZ Newschannel 3.

My head whipped around
like I heard the faint whisper
of a recent haint.
Great Mamaw
there in the backwoods banality
floating in the air.
Sure as the world she was there
and that two-tiered, big-ass,
blue-and-white umbrella was a sign,

sure as the world.
She always wanted to win it
and hear her name
pronounced on air
across the tri-state viewing area.

Truck Stop Strangers

I woke up with strangers on my mind.
Little flashes of the features
of the people my life collided with
when I worked third shift at a truck stop
in the middle of the Midwest.
Strangers I adopted as familiar faces
to get me through some lonely midnights
far from the hills and hollers of home.

Like the boys from the car wash next door
who made their money scrambling
over semis with soapy rags at top speeds,
even in the dead of winter when icicles
caked up their beards and sideburns
and their fingertips turned purple and blue.
They spent their money on lottery tickets
and Marlboro Reds and Nugget
and Mountain Dew.

Or the middle-aged waitress with sad eyes
who came in like clockwork
for a pack of Busch
and a half pint of Tvarsky, hundred proof.
Exhausted after an evening
of attending to lecherous drivers
and stingy tourists passing through,
she counted out dingy dollar bills
from her dingy apron pocket
and even her teased hair had fallen.
Wilted. Given up.

There was the big-bellied pig farmer
who ushered in the dawn
with a load of squealing hogs,
doomed and stacked three deep
in a shiny, silver trailer.
He stopped to fill up the gas tank
on the way to the slaughterhouse.

His leather face was smattered with grime
and laugh lines and grimaces,
spread out in equal parts.
He grumbled if my timing was off
and his coffee wasn't fresh enough.

I'll never forget the night
a girl I went to high school with
walked through the double doors.
She was great big pregnant
and on the arm of a truck-drivin' husband
and we both stopped to take stock,
incredulous that East Kentucky
could sashay in out of a cornfield
off the highway outside Kingdom City.

The Lilac Bush

I walked down in the holler
to visit Great Mamaw's house
and scour the cellar
and raid the lilac bush
growing bigger and bolder
and unfettered
in the front yard.
The lilac squeaks

and rains down dewdrops.
And I tell myself that they're tears of joy.
That the flowering bush I've known
and loved and tended to
is moved to be remembered.
To be plucked.
To drink sugar water in a vase
and fill the kitchen
with its sweet, sympathetic smell.

Wood Paneling

I keep on waking up
with my back against the wall.
Soft, smoldering, pale flesh
rubbed pink and raw and sensitive
by the rough wood paneling.
Raised stripes of skin stamped
on the backs of my thick thighs
and perfectly spaced.
I blink myself awake

and the boxy trailer bedroom
looks infinite and empty
instead of claustrophobic.
And I hate that blank, white sheet
and the way it looks like
my twin bed stretches out
toward a lonely eternity.
Half-asleep

I feel like I could reach out
and reach out
and reach out
and stretch myself out
across that sterile, cotton space
and still find nothing
to hold onto.

Blooms and the Blood

I ain't afraid of bumblebees
or the itchy aftermath of chigger weed.
The clover is too green.
Vibrantly begging to be disturbed.
And so I flop down on the ground.
Flat on my back and weak
against the temptation to feel
the earth enfold me,

hold me.
I smell lilies and chocolate mint
and honeysuckle vining high.
I feel the soil soak into my veins —
straight into my blood,
pumped into my heart.
I close my eyes
and feel the beat of it blooming
and remember
how you should only plant flowers
when the signs are in the reins.
Blossoms and bulbs are begat by blood.

Attempted Escape

The night Great Mamaw started fighting Death,
we walked and walked.
We paced the single-wide hallway
over and over and over again.
But we still couldn't get away.
I read the pamphlet left behind

by the pretty hospice nurse.
It was mint green with a ship
sailing off for some sketchy horizon.
I saved it in a shoe box
alongside letters from strangers
and Great Mamaw's spare pair of glasses.
I don't know why I saved it.
I read it

but it didn't register.
Confusion comes on first.
I couldn't match up the steps
in the pamphlet
with the struggle unfolding
as she paced in slow circles.
The thump and shuffle of her walker
mesmerized me as we moved
around and around the back bedroom,
up and down that hall.

And my Great Mamaw fought heroically.
Attempting her escape and casting me
as her terrified sidekick,
trying desperately
to make sense of the invisible enemy
forcing us to flee in circles.

Funeral Flowers

I've taken up residence
in her favorite chair.
I pulled it up by the roots
from its warm, cozy spot
in front of the stove
where it dented the carpet eternally.
I reset it deep in the far end of the kitchen
where the light is real good
amid the foliage of houseplants
and woods beyond the windows.
We're situated right on the ridgeline,

suspended over the holler
on top of a hilltop pushed flat enough
for the trailer to squat.
But the hill gets steep pretty quick
and the boughs of rough, black pine
and the slender needles of spruce
bob and bounce on a breeze
at the whim of cold wind.
Her funeral flowers won't grow
in the foothills.
They're hothouse flowers that fold
under the weight of winter
just around the bend.

Powerball Power Play

Y'all know what I'd do
with that Powerball money?
Billions of dollars.
Can you even imagine?
Five hundred bucks
tucked away in my two-dollar,
flea market wallet
would feel like five million to me.
Billionaires ain't people—
they're pasty, cutthroat creatures
of comfort.
But that's besides the point.
You know what I'd do?
I'll tell you what I'd do—

I'd own this whole damned county.
I'd buy out the good ol' boys
'cause I'm getting sicker and sicker
of them getting fatter and fatter
on donuts and government paychecks,
with a hot and hearty side
of homegrown nepotism.
I'd buy out the whole damned courthouse

and start my own one-woman
Stark Ridge super PAC
and install more suitable candidates,
handpicked by me
from hardscrabble dirt.
I'd donate so much money
to my old alma mater
they'd have to put my damned name on it.
And I'd give all the kids—

all the kids, every last one—
a chance.
In spite of their spot
in the country-ass caste system.
To spite it.
And you know what else?

I'd spend that dirty money
and own land.
I'd amass a fortress of forgotten farms
and old homeplaces abandoned
by greedy generations who'd rather
hunker down to die a slow death
of suburban boredom.
And then I'd give it all away.

It's their loss
and Powerball money well spent.

From around Here

I sprouted
from a hillbilly hoodoo garden
nurtured by the shining signs
in the stars
in the night sky,
tended to by the phases of the moon.
I bloomed, full, from superstition
from Mars
from timeless magic mothers
who wear the pants
and grow the food
and put it on the table.
I sprang up from the rich soil

and I busted up out of the dirty dirt.
I am a bastard born
of the lusty loins of a bad-boy hick
with a handsome, blond mustache.
I was conceived, unexpectedly,
in an encounter with a beautiful
kindhearted country girl.
I was created when opposites attracted
and connected and danced
and fell apart, together.

I kicked my way
out of a powerful
one-woman womb

at the end of a gravel road.
I burst from the belly
of a holler
in the sticks
in Kentucky.
I come hard
from laughter instead of tears,

from a place of mythic Mamaws
and Papaws
and kin thicker than blood
or water
or moonshine.
I descended from a change in elevation,

from thin, sweet air.
I found myself in tangles
of dogwood
and laurel
and sassafras
and hemlock.
I was swaddled
in the stout vines of honeysuckle
and I float still
on a cloud of monarch butterflies
fueled by the grape candy scent
of lilacs.

Picnicking with the Dead

The gravel road is so serene.
There's no lanes
and no lines
and no traffic.
Not a single car to steer clear of
coming out the ridge.
The crunch of rock
beneath my wheels
has rhythm.
In my dream

I feel peaceful.
And I'm on my way back
from the graveyard.
And the windows are down
and the steep curves
smell doused in honeysuckle
and the steering wheel
is hot in the palms
of my hands.
Summer is taking one last gasp
but in my dream

I'm not sweating.
And I'm on my way home
from a picnic
with the dead.